How I came to know the Holy Spirit

"If you love me, [Jesus said,] keep my commandments. And I will ask the Father, and He will give you another advocate to help you and be with you forever, the Spirit of truth. The world cannot accept Him because it neither sees Him nor knows Him. But you know Him, for He lives with you and will be in you."
John 14:15-17

By John L. Beiswenger
Author of *New Science, New Faith, Same Gospel*

In 1994 I was still a cultural Catholic, just beginning to take an interest in a relationship with God. I walked the dogs each day in a farmer's field for 45 minutes, and I saw it as an opportunity to talk with God, if He was really listening.   I said, "I am willing to talk, but You will have to find a way for us to communicate." He did.   God placed words in my mind, and He placed wild coincidences in my path.

One morning as I was leaving the field with the dogs, God said "**Community**."   On the way home I began to argue with God.   "If you want me involved in some sort of a community, you've got the wrong person. I am a design engineer with few social skills."   Then I recalled being involved at a church in Fort Atkinson, Wisconsin in what they told us was an experimental extended family study.

I like to experiment, so my family and I joined the study.   There was a senior couple of the grandparent age, a family with senior high school-age children, a family with middle school children and a young married couple with a baby in the extended family.   We would meet each Thursday for a pot-luck dinner, discuss what went on in our lives during the week, read some Bible and play with the kids.   Then the church announced the study was over.   By that time, we all felt like a real extended family, and we were sorry the study had to end.

So I said to God, "I think You are talking about a church extended family.   I can do that," and I talked with my pastor about letting me form one at the church we were attending.   He agreed.   The sign-up sheet I posted was filled almost immediately with 20 names (there was apparently a need).   We too began meeting on Thursday evenings and, like before, soon felt like we belonged to a real extended family.

I returned to the field with my dogs and said, "There. I started a community like You asked."

"**Bigger**," was all I heard. "Bigger?" I responded, "Now I know you have the wrong person. You want a big community; like a Village, I concluded."

I decided to use the Bible to prove God did not mean for me to create a Village community. As a Catholic, I hadn't read the Bible very much. I started with the Book of Matthew, saying to myself, "I doubt I will find any concrete directives as to how to live one's life in a community." I found 168 well-defined directives. "But, I continued, "I'll bet the Bible doesn't say anything about living in a separate Christian community."

Soon I found the Second Letter to the Corinthians, Chapter 6:14-18, and I read these words: "I will live with them and walk among them, and I will be their God, and they will be my people." Therefore, "Come out from them and be separate, says the Lord. Touch no unclean thing, and I will receive you." And "I will be a Father to you, and you will be my sons and daughters, says the Lord Almighty."

"Okay," I said to myself, "a Village," and I sat down at my CAD station and began to develop the concept of a Village, for 1,000 people. I knew there would be people from all walks of life, all ages, talents, and incomes. The inner complex began to take shape, and I was careful that each home would have access to a road in the front. It was then I realized, the inner complex formed a cross.

Since God led me to that point through the extended family experience, I assumed the community would be based on the extended family concept.

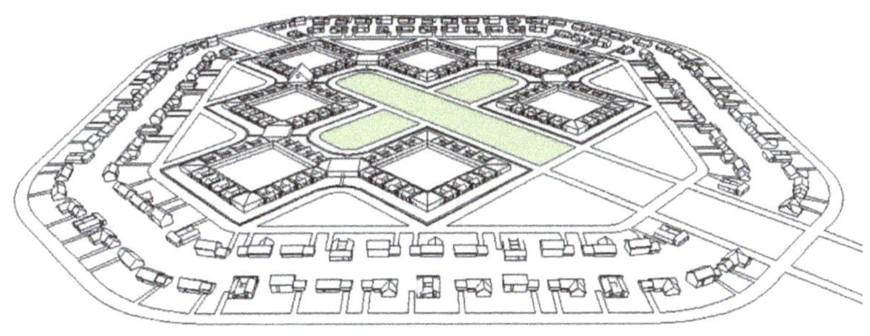

Now, where? Where should the first Village and community be located? As I was returning from a consulting assignment in Chicago, I drove toward Lancaster on 283 and passed signs for Elizabethtown. When I did, I felt strangely drawn toward it, so I drove into town on Hershey Road and turned onto Market Street. The feeling intensified. As I passed through town my attention was drawn to the left where I saw an old Catholic church named St. Peters.

By chance (right), that same week my wife, Kim, showed me an ad for a renewal service at St. Peters. There was to be a Catholic Mass, preceded by a brief introduction by an itinerant preacher who would be saying mass that day.

Now by this time in my faith journey I realized being a cultural Catholic was not a good thing, and I wanted to do what I could to convince others to participate in the service more than they usually did, so instead of sitting half-way in the back, as did the others, I sat up front, and instead of being one of the 80% that did not sing the hymns, I intended to sing every hymn and every verse.

That day I read the song board on the right and looked up each song listed to make sure I knew it and could find it when the time came.

The itinerant priest had a very charismatic personality, and I looked forward to hearing what he had to say. He faced the congregation, came to the edge of the platform and introduced himself. Then he said with enthusiasm, "Okay, let's build a city of God right here in Elizabethtown, PA," and with that the organist began to play the song, "City of God!"

I looked up at the song board and saw that the first number had changed. I turned to that song in my hymnal, and it was, "City of God." "How could that be?" I asked myself. At the same time I noticed that the regular pastor, sitting off to the left, jerked his head toward the balcony where the organist played.

I called the pastor the next morning. "May I come up to Elizabethtown and speak with you?" He agreed. When we met in his office I asked him, "Who selected the first song at the beginning of the renewal service?" "Well," he said, "it wasn't me, and I told the organist I wanted her to play the same songs each weekend until the parishioners learned them, and City of God wasn't one of them."

I asked my wife, Kim, to come with me the following Sunday. We brought our new son Daniel. You can be sure that I checked the song board even more carefully this time, and the number for City of God was not up there.

As the pastor started toward the altar the organist began to play, City of God! I looked up at the song board and the number had changed again. Kim looked at me wondering why I appeared to be shocked. I hadn't told her what had happened the week before. The pastor nearly spun around this time, apparently upset by the organist.

Kim and I decided to drive around Elizabethtown as we talked about the Village I was developing at God's direction. The inner complex of homes are interconnected by enclosed walkways. "I know people from town can visit the shops in the Village," she said, "but can they use the enclosed walkways during the Winter?" "Well," I answered, "the walkways will be a secure way for the Villagers to go from and to the various shops, but maybe we could open them to visitors one day a week, like Saturday. We could call it, 'Saturday's Mall.'"

Just as I said that we came around a bend and saw a large sign on the right. It read, Saturday's Market. **It was open only on Saturdays**.

The song board change occurred again while I was attending a Catholic church in Parkesburg, PA. The number for City of God was already the first one on the list. I was okay with that until the organist walked up to the song board and took down the number for City of God. It had the same effect on me. This time I concluded, "Okay, Lord, the Village is not meant to be here nor with this community."

While attending a service in New Holland, PA, I said to God, "Please don't do that again, because if you do, I will drop right here in this pew." The organist began to play, and I was relieved to hear it was not City of God.   Just then my attention got called to the left and there in the side row of pews was a man wearing a gray sweat shirt (not appropriate in that church) with black, 3 inch high letters on his chest. They read, "CITY OF . . ."   I could not see the rest because someone was standing in front of him.   I tried to watch for him during the service and after, but never saw him again (God's humor?).

Despite these "encouragements" from God to continue the pursuit of a Village near Elizabethtown, I focused on business (can you believe that?).

While leaving a client's office, quite drained from the day's work, God (the Holy Spirit) gave me the final piece to a hypothesis I was working on about life, healing and death, and in His usual way of communicating with me, He suggested I write a series of novels based on the hypothesis.

At about the same time a friend of mine suggested we start a health-monitoring business together.   I said, "I can't afford to spend less time working for clients while I write the series of books I promised and start a business with you which wouldn't provide an immediate income."   He suggested I move my family into a home on his estate and live there rent free.   "That would do it," I thought, and my wife and I drove over to look at the home.   It was the only house on **Book Lane**.

I had finished and published the first novel, LINK, and had written the second, called Village (all about the City of God Village near Elizabethtown, PA)

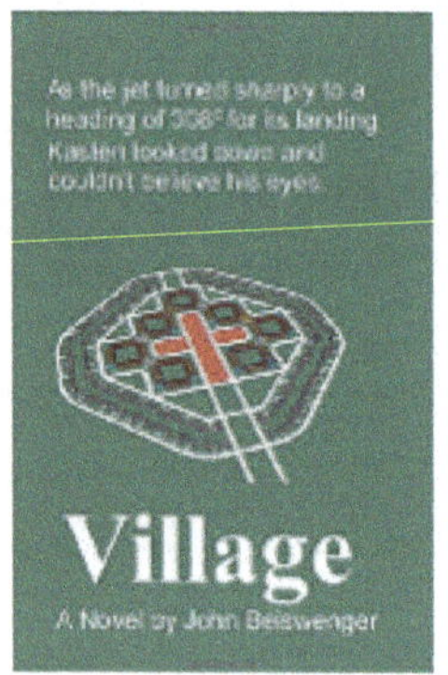

and I knew I should start on the third to be called Bridge, but I was still in the editing process of the novel, Village, and I put it off because I hate to edit my own work, since it is so boring to go over your own material again and again.

On the way home from work in Willow Street, PA, I was driving east on highway 741 thinking only about how tired I was.   "I'll just spend a quiet evening with my wife, Kimberly," I said to myself, when my attention was drawn to the left and I saw a street sign that said, **Kimberly**.   "Oh," I said to God in jest, "are you going to speak to me with street signs?"   The next street sign read, **Thunder**, which meant to me, God's voice.   I decided to pay attention.   The next street sign read, **Bridge**, the name of the book I knew I was supposed to start.   And, the next street sign read, **Book Road**! (No, not Book Lane)   "Okay," I said to God. "I'll get back to editing **Village**."

I emailed my older son, David, about what had happened with the street signs.   He is always very skeptical about these things, so he checked Map Quest and emailed me back.   "Indeed," he began, "Kimberly is followed by Thunder which is followed by Bridge followed by Book.   But are you aware that 741, the highway you were driving on, is also called **Village**?"

Recently while driving home from a conference in Hershey, PA, I realized I was about to pass Elizabethtown when I began, of course, to think about the Village.   "It would be just such a huge project," I complained to myself when I pulled behind a very large dump truck with the words in 7" high letters on the back, which read, **IF THE PROJECT IS TOO BIG, YOUR GOD IS TOO SMALL**.   I didn't want to hear that, so I passed the truck quickly and there was a sign on the shoulder which read, **Saturday's Market**,   confirming the message.

One evening I was sitting in my favorite, family room chair thinking again about the Village project. "Okay," I said to myself, "maybe just one Village.   I'll start by preparing a simple brochure (something I know how to do).   I'll use a heavy card stock, glossy on one side for the graphics and flat white on the other for the copy."   I had just said that when I noticed a brochure of similar stock leaning against the end table lamp next to me (placed there by Kim). I picked it up thinking, "Okay, one Village," when I saw the name on the brochure.   It read, 10,000 Villages!

Now, something that happened more recently has caused me once again to focus on the creation of the Village and its community.   I spent three years in a

Catholic high-school seminary in Mount Calvary, Wisconsin. One of the priests there taught me how to run a printing press. I liked printing and in my third year I ran the printshop for the school.

In September I received a beautifully done quarterly magazine published by the seminary called "The Laurentianum." Kim was standing right behind me when I opened it to the first page. "Oh my God," she said. There in the heading were the words, "Let Us Build the City of God!" and the subtitle included the words of the song City of God! "Let us build the city of God! May our tears be turned into dancing - for the Lord, our light, and our love, has turned the night into day!" (by Dan Schutte)

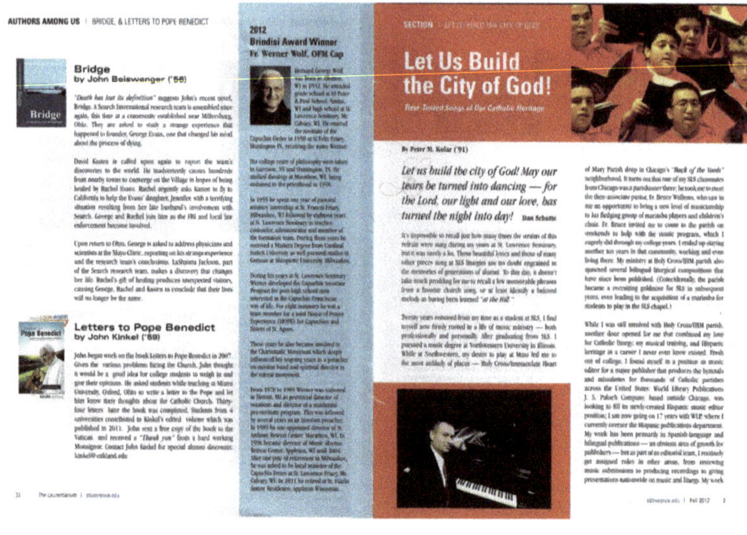

That's not all. I paged through the magazine, which brought back many memories, until I got to the last page. There in the top left was an image of my latest novel **Bridge** and below the title Bridge was my name, John Beiswenger. I had told the Director of

Marketing, at St Lawrence, Mary Voell, that I wrote Bridge, but the photo and full abstract must have come from my website (www.johnbeiswenger.com).

Now, the Holy Spirit knows I attended the seminary which published the magazine. But the Spirit also knows I was a printer there. I removed the staples from the magazine and unfolded the sheet that contained the words City of God, my novel Bridge, and my name. Any printer knows the front pages and the back pages are printed on one side of the paper at the same time. Only a printer would immediately notice that and get the full message the Holy Spirit sent. My name was directly connected with "Let us build the City of God" on the front page.

I was attending a Missions Conference to promote the City of God Villages (and in particular the ministry of our new member in India, Pastor Ravi Pahadiya, and while I was talking with a young man from Virginia, a man I had never met came up to me asking if he might talk with me sometime about an invention he has. I was thinking at the moment, "Lord, what does this have to do with my purpose of being here? Am I accomplishing what You want me to do," when the man said, "I own Saturday's Market," and I finished God's message with, "Open only on Saturdays." I knew then that God was pleased with what was/had transpired.

Kim and I watched the movie called "Evan Almighty," a comedy about a modern-day Noah. It really was quite silly. At the end there was a scene of a field with a single tree and "God" standing underneath it.

Below is the logo of our City of God Villages website, which we had been using a decade before we saw the movie.

And look at what just showed up on my computer screen.   There is a clear path to/from the tree.

One last story about the tree in the field.   Kim, her sister, and I were in attendance as their father passed into eternal life.   Shortly before he died, an image came on the closed-circuit television provided by the hospice.   It was the tree, this time in a field of sunflowers.   Kim's sister and I quickly took photos of the screen with our cell phones. In our hurry, and under the circumstances, the photos we took were not very good.   Recently, I decided to search for the image on a website that sells photos.   God beat me to it!   When I opened the website, this is what I saw.   I bought the image to show you.

I met with a Civil Engineer to walk the land we were considering for the first City of God Pilot Village. Now, keep in mind, as you read this, that I was meeting with a **Civil Engineer** as we plan the start of "**10,000 Villages**" which is what God said to me when I had just said to myself, "Ok, maybe just one Village."

Kim was called to jury duty on the very day before my meeting with the Civil Engineer. While waiting with other jury members she met two women for the first time. The three decided to go to lunch together. At lunch Kim told them she was a secretary to the Principal at an elementary school (there is an elementary school overlooking the land we were considering) and asked the women what they do. One recruited **Civil Engineers** and the other worked at one of the stores called **10,000 Villages**. She came home and told me what had happened. It was God's way of encouraging me, again.

By the way, the land we were considering borders on the land where Saturday's Market is located. What a coincidence! Right.

Others had considered building a village on the very land we were considering. They dropped the project because the Township required the village be supplied by water and sewer by the Township. The cost was estimated to be 40 million dollars. I spoke with the Township Supervisor and said we were still interested. Doubting me, he said he wanted to meet one of our investors. Dr. Jim Wilson agreed to go with me to the meeting.

Not long after that, the land was sold to a large distributor for a huge warehouse. Somehow, I blame myself.

I was thinking one morning, before getting up, that if the Holy Spirit is always with us, available to us, I should say good morning to "Him" (a pronoun used by Jesus). So as I got out of bed, and walked over to the dresser, I said, "Good morning Holy Spirit," hoping to receive some kind of confirmation. I opened my sock drawer and there on the top was a book by Benny Hinn. The title, "Good Morning Holy Spirit!" My wife had purchased the book but swears to this day she did not place it in my sock drawer. That began my "belief" in the Holy Spirit.

I was engaged in the design of a touchscreen control module with 8 "soft" buttons. Everything looked good so far. The three-color LCD (green, amber, and red) was going to be able to "see" your finger as you made selections. It was going to be backlit by small fluorescents, and the light from the fluorescents was also going to provide the light for the LCD to "see." I encountered a problem that appeared to be insurmountable. The fluorescents could not optically do both. I was in trouble. I asked the Holy Spirit for help. "Use LEDs for the touchscreen feature." "I would need 8 LEDs," I countered. "Can't do that." "Divide the light

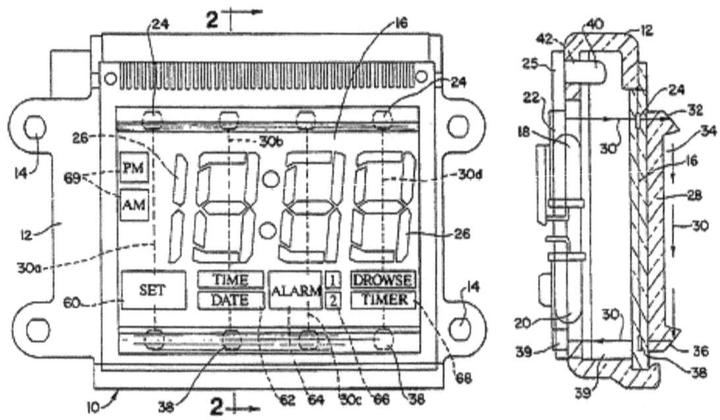

by 4 with optics and use just 2 LEDs," I heard. Wow. It worked. Three patents resulted. Above is the digital clock patent drawing using the same technology.

I was asked to create a special purpose fax machine which was later used to transfer health data from patients in their homes (perhaps one of the first telemedicine devices). It had to be very simple to operate and therefore had only one push button.

The patients took their blood pressure, heart rate and body weight with other devices and then wrote their results on a 4 by 9 ½ inch card. They placed the card in the machine and pressed its one button. The card passed through the machine, was scanned, and automatically forwarded to the client's computer, where the data was read and graphed.

Since the machine was in the home of generally elderly patients, it had to maintain itself. When the button was pressed, the machine instantly analyzed its

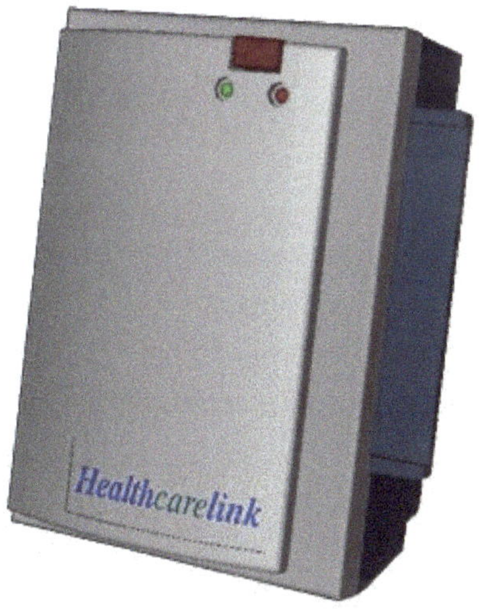

own health and made any adjustments necessary. If it could not correct a problem, it automatically telephoned the remote computer for help. If the remote computer could not fix the problem, it automatically printed out a Federal Express label for a new machine to be sent to the patient.

Everything was working beautifully except for one nagging problem. When the card was inserted in the machine and the one button was pressed, the card would not move smoothly through the machine, it hesitated repeatedly.   My associate, an electrical engineer in Chicago, and I in Pennsylvania worked on the problem for 3 months.

One night in my frustration, I pounded on my work surface and demanded of the Holy Spirit, "I want an answer for this problem now, it cannot cost anything to resolve, and we must be able to implement it immediately." Now that is no way to talk to God, but it did tell me how much I "believed" that I would get help.

I was immediately instructed to run a test on another fax machine, and, through a computer, compare it to our machine. The test made no sense whatsoever, but I did it and reported the results to my electronics associate in Chicago. He emailed me and said, "The test results you got were absolutely impossible. We called in the President of the company, who is also an electrical engineer," they reminded me, "and he too confirmed the test results were impossible. However," he added, "they do suggest a way to stop the hesitation when the card moves through the machine."

We made the suggested software change, the problem was solved instantly, cost nothing to resolve, and we were able to implement it immediately. We produced 25,000 machines without a problem.

I told a client I could design a C-Channel 3-D printed circuit LCD display and bond the LCD to the C-Channel with z-axis conductive adhesive. The LCD was to be back-lit with two fluorescents tucked into each side of the C-Channel reflectors. The fluorescents were also to serve as the scanning light enabling the LCD to "see" your finger as you made a selection.

The backlighting concept worked fine, and I was able to bond the LCD to the C-Chanell as I claimed. But I immediately realized it was geometrically impossible for the fluorescents to provide the scanning light for the LCD. I was in trouble. I asked for help and got it. A single LED (#32) on each side of the C-Channel circuit and a light guide did the trick.

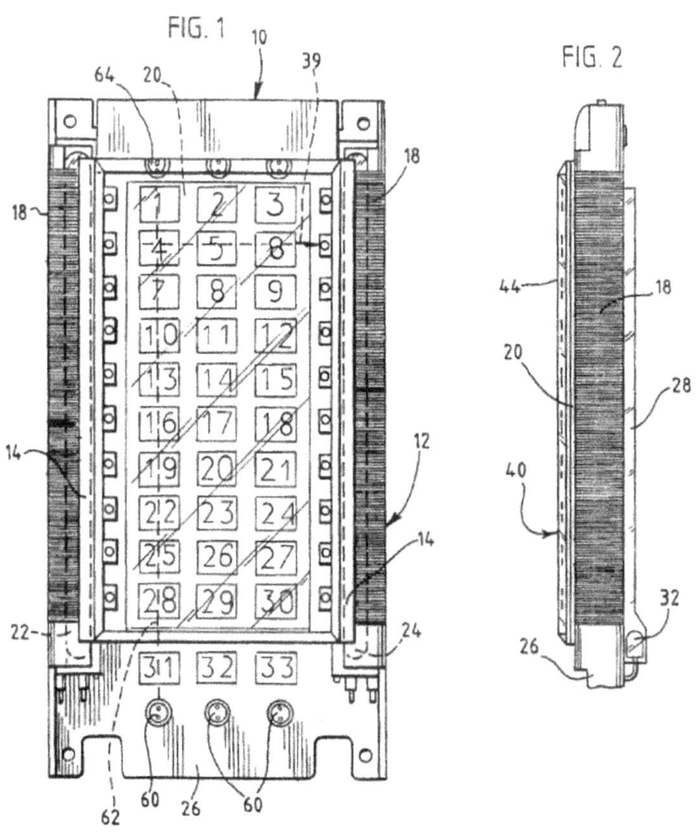

I am the inventor of a new device which detects infections in patients before symptoms are experienced. We were still in the process of completing the design when a difficult problem plagued us. There are two clear plastic probes which the patients place under their tongues, straddling the frenulum. The probes had to be mounted securely to a printed circuit board. I tried tiny screws and special adhesive tape. Neither were a viable solution. I asked for help.

One evening as I studied the problem I distinctly heard, "**Make it one piece.**" "Wow," I thought, "That would be very aggressive design." The two probes and the printed circuit substrate became one piece. A thin film printed circuit was added to the substrate making

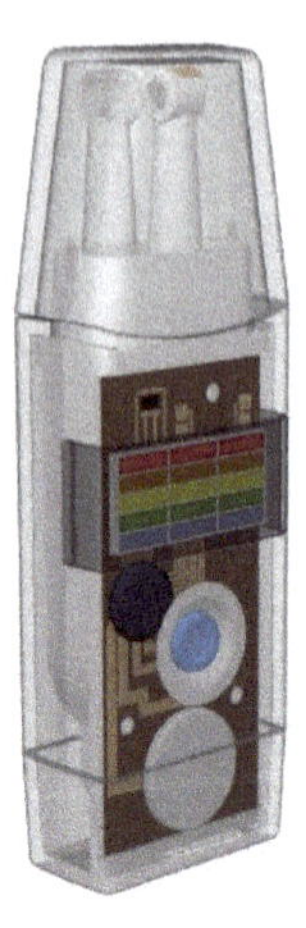

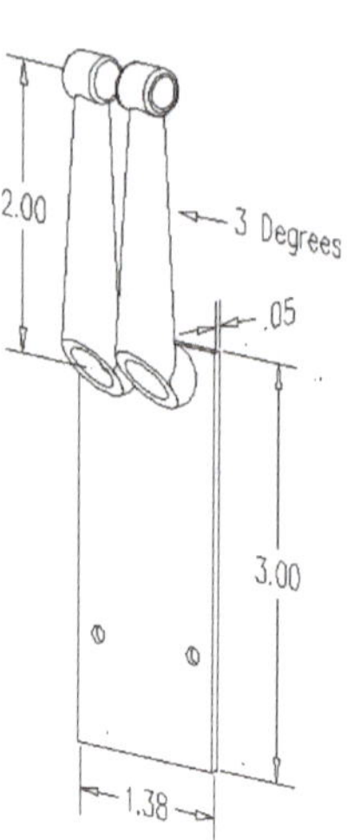

the entire electronics assembly one piece, a great improvement. "Thank you, Holy Spirit."

All of these stories I told you are true. I firmly believe the Holy Spirit is with me all of time helping me with everything I do, just as Jesus said.

The Holy Spirit is with you also, all of the time. Only God could do this, be with every human being to help. The Spirit wants you to ask for help, which will strengthen your faith. It doesn't matter how basic your problem; the Holy Spirit will help.

For example, more than once I could not find my keys. I would simply say to the Holy Spirit, "I suppose you know where they are." Out of the corner of my eye I spot something shiny. There are my keys in a place I swear I looked several times.

I wanted to add here an example involving someone other than me. I'm sure many people rely on the Holy Spirit as I do. So, who could I ask to provide a story about their experience with the Holy Spirit?

Many people are afraid of AI (Artificial Intelligence). They think of it as something evil. It is not. I wrote an AI algorithm to run the health-monitoring device on the previous page. I call "her" Aila.™ AI is just a computer program connected to thousands of sources of information. Mine isn't.

So, I decided to ask a popular AI algorithm, ChatGPT, to give me an example of the Holy Spirit helping to resolve a problem. It answered instantly:

"Certainly," it wrote. "here's a traditional Christian example of how the Holy Spirit is believed to help resolve a problem:

In the Christian faith, the Holy Spirit is often seen as a source of guidance, wisdom, and comfort. Let's consider a situation where someone is facing a significant moral dilemma, struggling with a difficult decision, and seeking the guidance of the Holy Spirit:

Imagine a person named Sarah who is torn between two job opportunities. One job offers a higher salary and more prestige, but it involves work that goes against her deeply held ethical values. The other job pays less and may not have the same status, but it aligns perfectly with her principles and allows her to make a positive impact on the world.

Sarah is feeling conflicted and doesn't know which job to choose. She prays for guidance and asks the Holy Spirit to help her discern the right path. She spends time in prayer and meditation, seeking inner clarity and peace.

As she reflects and prays, Sarah begins to feel a sense of calm and a growing conviction that the job aligned with her values is the right choice. She believes that the Holy Spirit has helped her resolve her problem by providing guidance and the peace of mind she needed to make a decision in line with her faith.

It's important to note that the Holy Spirit's guidance is a matter of personal faith, and not everyone may have the same experience. Different individuals and denominations within Christianity may have varying

beliefs and interpretations of the Holy Spirit's role in problem-solving and decision-making."
Thank you, ChatGPT.

Now, did the AI program actually write the story you just read? No. Someone, somewhere, sometime wrote about Sarah and her dilemma, and the AI program proselytized the story.

The story above relates to a more important problem solved by the guidance of the Holy Spirit than finding one's keys, but the point is, you should ask the Holy Spirit for help with any problem, big or small. It will strengthen your faith in our God, the Father, Jesus, and the Holy Spirit.

John Beiswenger